MW00778596

Prayer

J O U R N E Y

BY SUE DOWNING

Cold Tree Press

Nashville, Tennessee

Library of Congress Number: 2006932463

Published by Cold Tree Press
Nashville, Tennessee
www.coldtreepress.com

Printed in the United States of America
ISBN 1-58385-084-8

In loving memory of my Mom
Verl Baumgartner
Fondly known as Gram
"Have a Happy"

Show gratitude along the way.

Acknowledgements

Dear Lord,

$\mathcal{I}$ come to you with a thankful heart for each person who helped make Prayer Journey a reality.

Praise and thanks to you for Paula Harris and Janice Elmore whose computer skills gave form and order to this book.

Praise and thanks to you for Bettye Malone whose beautiful watercolor painting graces the cover of Prayer Journey.

Praise and thanks to you for my publisher, Peter Honsberger of Cold Tree Press, for his commitment to quality and dedication to his authors.

Praise and thanks to you for my husband Jim for his loving support every step of the way.

Praise and thanks to you for our infant son Scottie who was the beginning of my journey with prayer.

Praise and thanks to you for my Mom. Her life continues to be an inspiration to me.

Lord, I come to you with a thankful heart.

I lift up my thanks and praise to you for these prayers, for they are your words not mine.

To you God, be the glory.

Amen

Forward

*I*n the journey of life there are tears and laughter, heartaches and happiness, ordinary days and birthdays. We who believe in God need effective ways to offer all these experiences to the Lord in prayer. In this book, Sue Downing has given us a tool for this purpose. Out of her own joys and sorrows, highs and lows, prayers and reflections, she brings us into the presence of the One who loves us unconditionally and supports us unendingly.

It is my distinct privilege to be Sue's pastor. I have been the recipient of some of these prayers. Sue has prayed them on my behalf. They have comforted me in sorrow, empowered me in ministry, and deepened my relationship with God. Sue is one of those persons who speaks with integrity when she says, "I am praying for you." Her compassionate spirit, her sensitive concern, her authentic spirituality is evident in all she does. Sue not only writes about prayer; she prays!

So let these words become expressions of your thoughts as you talk with the Lord about your journey of life. All of us were born.

Everybody has a birthday. Morning never wears to evening but some heart breaks, a heart just as sensitive as yours and mine. In all these seasons of life, we long to communicate with God. Thanks to Sue, we now have words which express the desires of our hearts.

J. Howard Olds
Senior Pastor
Brentwood United Methodist Church
Brentwood, Tennessee

And He walks with me, and He talks with me, and He tells me I am his own.

Preface

Dear Friends,

Prayer Journey begins with a personal story; a story of God's abundant and everlasting love; a story that forever changed my life; a story that helped shape the prayers of this book.

SCOTTIE'S BOX

Gently, I lift the box off the shelf of our bedroom closet. It is a large Christmas box covered with brightly colored, smiling angels which children have drawn. I set the box down and carefully remove its lid to evoke once more the flood of memories stored here.

This is not the first, nor will it be the last time I will repeat these familiar steps. The corners of the box are torn from the bulging contents within. The angels gracing the box do not shine quite as brightly as they used to; however the memories this box holds are so vividly etched in my heart and mind; it is as if they only occurred yesterday.

It came into being twenty-seven years ago when our son Scottie was born. The box's value is immeasurable. It radiates and overflows with tangible evidence of God's abundant love. Scottie's box is filled with gentle, yet powerful, reminders of how God works through others in our darkest hours, to touch us with love when we are hurting.

I invite you now to walk with me through Scottie's box and let me share with you a beautiful story of God's love. My eyes fall upon a birth certificate for James Scott Downing, born March 5, 1979. Along with it is a hospital crib card announcing," It's a boy!" As I view these things, my thoughts carry me back to the time of Scottie's life on earth; a time which would forever impact the lives of me, my husband Jim, and our daughter Julie, who was four years old when her brother was born.

It was a very normal, uneventful pregnancy, with no indication there could be any problem. When I was wheeled into the delivery room at Fort Sanders Hospital in Knoxville, Tennessee, on March 5, 1979, I felt only joyful anticipation at the birth of our second child. Scottie was born with spina bifida, an opening of the spine. As our doctor told us the following morning, Scottie's case was one of the worst ever encountered. In addition, Scottie was hydro-cephalic, and his brain was almost entirely fluid. The prognosis was very bleak.

Amidst the shock, denial, loneliness, and intense pain we felt, Jim and I reached out to God through prayer in a way we never had before. Thanks to our parents, Jim and I had been exposed to the influence of the church. Our parents had also set a loving Christian example at home for us to follow. Shortly after Scottie's birth, Jim put his arms around his parents and said, "Mom, Dad, isn't this what you have always taught me, to trust God? God has given us this little boy, and God will help us to care for him." As I reflect on this tragic time in our lives, I am convinced we could not have survived without the seeds of faith our parents helped to instill in us and without the gift of overwhelming love we received.

In the days following Scottie's birth, God was unmistakably there. Jim, our four-year old daughter Julie, and I received such all-encompassing love it could have only come from God. Family and friends were always on hand. The outpouring of love from our church is difficult to describe. Our Cokesbury Church family provided us with meals. Our minister, Jerry Anderson was there whenever we needed him.

I pause in my thoughts to explore Scottie's box further. It reveals a church newsletter telling about a newly formed Sunday School class at Cokesbury United Methodist Church that was named in honor of Scottie.

As I delve deeper into our box, I am made aware yet again of the countless number of people who took the time to send cards, notes, and letters to let us know we were not alone. Twenty-seven years later, these cherished messages of love continue to offer comfort.

On Tuesday, April 3, 1979, twenty-nine days after his birth, Scottie died. We were surrounded by family and friends. Julie was there too. I remember Jim looking at her, tears glistening in his eyes, and saying, "Punkin, Scottie's gone. We'll not see him again." "Oh, yes we will, Daddy," she said. "We'll see him when we get to heaven." What a source of comfort these words have been over the years!

Scottie was buried on Thursday, April 5. Here before me is our copy of the message from Scottie's memorial service which was centered on I Corinthians 13, Paul's great poem on love. As I glance at the text I am struck again by these words of our then pastor. "In the few short weeks of Scottie's life, he has opened doors to an outpouring of love in our church and community. A little child has led us into new dimensions of real loving and caring, and because of that we will never be the same."

After Scottie's death, the Lord continued to wrap his loving arms around us in many ways. I also had a growing desire to give to God in every way I could and pass on to others the love we were so generously receiving. I prayed to the Lord for guidance. I had no baby to care for as I had expected, and Julie was headed for kindergarten. "Use me, Lord." I prayed. Thus began my ongoing ministry with children and the discovery of my God-given gift to write, both which continue to bless my life abundantly. Prayer Journey, as well as my other writings, grew out of this very special time in my life. It is an outpouring of love that comes from my heart. I invite you to step with me now as we walk, together with God, through the prayers of this book.

— Sue Downing
Scottie's Mom

Table of Contents

JOURNEY

BY SUE DOWNING

Pray along the way.

Pray along the way.

A Life of Prayer

*L*ord,

Teach me to walk with you.

Let all my life be a living prayer for you.

Enlighten my heart that prayer is

Speaking, listening,

Whispering, shouting,

Thinking, singing,

Laughing, crying,

Prayer is this and even more.

Prayer is

Bowing heads, folding hands,

Kneeling, sitting,

Standing, walking,

Dancing, running,

Reaching, touching,

Prayer is this and even more.

Prayer is

> Thanking, praising,
>
> Giving, receiving,
>
> Questioning, believing,
>
> Caring, forgiving
>
> Hoping, growing,
>
> Grieving, rejoicing,
>
> Anticipating, remembering,
>
> Prayer is this and even more.

> Prayer is your precious gift to us.
>
> Prayer is choosing the abundant life.
>
> Prayer is never being alone.
>
> Prayer is a journey:
>
> > a journey of love with you God.

Amen

Take time for meditation along the way.

Take time for meditation along the way.

Commune with God

I prepare.

Lord, help me to be still and know that you are God.

Free my mind from all those needless thoughts and clutter

that hinder my focus on you.

Let me feel your loving arms drawing me close.

Let me hear your voice calling me.

Permeate my whole being with your spirit.

Fill me with that inner peace which can only come from you.

I give thanks and praise.

Lord, illumine my heart with all the blessings that are mine.

Listen, as I name them one by one,

with praise and thanksgiving to you.

I lift up others.

Lord, I bring these persons before you in prayer.

Show me how I can be your instrument of love to each one.

I ask forgiveness.

Lord, I come to your communion table and partake of the bread

and wine, your body broken for me, your blood poured out for me.

Rekindle in me the truth that you gave your son, Jesus, for my sins.

I kneel at the cross and confess these sins, to you.

I cast my cares upon you.

Lord, these heavy burdens weigh me down.

I cannot handle them on my own.

I relinquish control and place them in your hands.

I follow.

Lord, help me to place you at the center and

seek out your will for my life.

Reveal to me how I can use my special gifts for your glory.

Grant me a listening heart and the desire to be your disciple.

I act.

Lord, when I leave this holy place, I pray that my actions

will reflect your love and spread your Word.

Let me serve you.

Let me experience the abundant life!

Amen

Sacrifice along the way.

Our Gifts to God

*L*ord,
 We are being asked to give; to make a commitment
to your church.

Guide us in the understanding that we are a fellowship
 of believers, a community of faith, bound together for
 the common purpose of glorifying you in all we do.

Impress on our hearts that the offering of our gifts is not for
 the few to pledge, but a shared responsibility and journey of
 each member.

Let us feel the willingness to sacrifice.
Let us feel the willingness to give.

Lord,

We are being asked to give.

Fill us with the deep desire to place your needs above ours.

Help us to carefully examine our lives and clearly envision
the contribution we are able to make.
Instill within us the tremendous importance and lasting impact
of our decision.
Let us feel the willingness to sacrifice.
Let us feel the willingness to give.

Lord,
We are being asked to give.
Impart to us the realization that the immediate choices we make
will affect not only the church now, but for generations to come.
Empower us to fulfill the vision we have to touch hearts
and transform lives.
Let us feel the willingness to sacrifice.
Let us feel the willingness to give.

Lord,
We are being asked to give; to make a commitment to your church.
We see your son Jesus dying on the cross for our sins,
giving us the gift of eternal life.
We worship a God who made the ultimate sacrifice for us.
What can we do in return?

Let us lovingly sacrifice.

Let us freely give.

Let us rejoice and give thanks for our blessings!

Praise be to God!

Amen

Have faith along the way.

Have faith along the way.

The Community of Faith

Lord, we pray for faith.
A faith that takes us beyond our fears,
A faith that gives us the courage to commit,
A faith that moves us out of complacency into action,
A faith that instills within us a willingness to risk,
A faith that places our complete trust in you, Lord,
A faith that says, "Here I am, Lord, use me!"

Lord, we pray for faith.
Guide us as we strive to reach out to others.
Empower us to love and minister in your name.
Empower us to become the community of faith
  you would have us to be.

Lord, we pray for faith.
We claim your promise that if we have faith as little as a grain
  of mustard seed, we can accomplish great things through you.

Help us to recognize the faith of all those before us that
brought your church to this point.

Help us to realize the tremendous privilege and responsibility
entrusted to us!

Lord, we pray for faith.

Guide us as we strive to reach out to others.

Empower us to love and minister in your name.

Empower us to become the community of faith
you would have us be.

Amen

Serve with gladness
along the way.

Serve with gladness along the way.

Going Forth

*L*ord, wrap your loving arms around your servants
    as they go forth.
Walk with them as they journey from this place in loving
    ministry for you.
Take their hands as they reach out to touch your children.
Help them to focus on the road ahead, and give them
    a clear vision of the needs you place before them.
Grant them the faith to embrace the future with hope
    and the assurance that they are never alone.

Wrap your loving arms around your servants as they go forth.
Walk with them as they journey from this place in loving
    ministry for you.
Open wide their hearts to receive and to take with them
    all the love and thanksgiving we carry in our hearts for them.
May they always remember what a precious gift they have been
    to each one of us.

May the cherished memories of experiences we have
  shared together go with them.

Wrap your loving arms around your servants as they go forth.

Walk with them as they journey from this place in loving
  ministry for you.

Watch over them as step by step they move forward
  to another place.

A place that will surely be enriched and blessed by their presence.

A place where your servants are surely an answer to prayer.

Amen

Let go along the way.

Let go along the way.

Hold Me Close

*L*ord Jesus,
   Wrap your loving arms around me and hold me close
so that I can let go.

Help me to loosen the grip I have on unwarranted
   anger, grudges I cling to, resentment, prejudice, and wrongs
      committed against me.

Pry away my hold onto materialism, love of power, self-centeredness,
   and the need to be in control.
Release my grasp from the burden of past sins,
   words spoken without thought, and actions taken too hastily.

Hold me close so that I can let go.
Carry me to your table where I partake of the bread and wine;
   your body broken for me, your blood shed for me.
Impress on my heart that your forgiveness is there for me.

Wrap your loving arms around me and hold me close,
so that I can let go and be lifted up by your
everlasting love and amazing grace.

Amen

*Discover God
along the way.*

God with Me

Almighty God,
As I journey through life,
I lift up my heartfelt thanks to you that

In a world of inevitable change and unpredictability,
you are constant.

In a world of fear and trepidation, you are peace.

In a world of greed and lust for power, you are strength.

In a world of oppression and despair, you are hope.

In a world of evil and hatred, you are love.

In a world of unfulfilled dreams and discouragement,
you are light.

In a world of sin and strife, you are forgiveness.

In a world of unworthiness and lack of gratitude,
you are grace.

In a world of false idols and misguided priorities,
you are the way.

In a world of wrong and injustice, you are goodness.

In a world of loneliness and separation, you are there.

Lord, as I journey through life draw me close to you,

  keep me by your side, and do not let me stray.

In the midst of this world I pray to discover you.

In the midst of this world I pray that my life will forever reflect you.

Amen

Find peace along the way.

Gift of Peace

Lord,
I pray for peace. I pray for the presence of your peace in my life.

Still my trembling spirit, and bathe me in the light of your love.

Silence the clamor all around me so that I can listen to your leading.

Free me from the relentless grip of greed, self-centeredness, hatred, and apathy.

Instill within my heart a faith that stands strong in the face of confusion, fear, adversity, despair, and wickedness.

I pray for peace. I pray for the presence of your peace in my life.

I pray for a peace filled with the passion to discern and act on your will.

I pray for a peace that allows me to face the very things that would rob me of this precious gift.

Lord,

I pray for peace. I pray for the presence of your peace in the world.

I pray for a peace filled with the passion to discern and act
   on your will.

I pray for a peace that allows each one of us to face the very things
   that would rob the world of this precious gift.

Oh, Lord, let it begin with me!

Amen

Listen along the way.

A Time to Listen

Lord,
 When others speak to me in their hurt and pain,
when they share their innermost feelings with me,

Let me listen with love.

Let me hear with my heart.

Clear my mind of unnecessary "clutter" that would hinder my
 ability to listen.

Take away the urge I might have to interrupt with my own
 solutions and answers.

Help me to focus completely on what is being said.

Prevent me from being judgmental.

Free me from my own agenda.

Oh, that my silence would reflect genuine care and compassion,

Oh, that I would listen as I wish others would listen to me.

Lord,

Let me listen with love,

Let me hear with my heart.

May I realize that listening is a choice I make; a precious gift to give.

May I know that the only way I can truly listen to others

 is by opening my heart to your word and your guidance first.

Fill me with your spirit, Lord.

Oh, that my listening would reflect you.

Oh, that I would listen to others as you listen to me.

Amen

Smile along the way.

Smile along the way.

A Happy Heart

Dear God,
 Put a smile on my face, laughter within my heart,
 and joy in my soul!

May I be generous with my smiles, giving these
 precious gifts of love often.

May I smile without being selective, realizing that all
 God's children need the warmth a smile can give.

May I willingly perform this small act of kindness, knowing the
 impact on another could be great.

Put a smile on my face, God!

Let there be laughter within my heart.

May I seek out times for laughter, knowing its wonderful capacity
 to heal and restore.

May I engage in laughter with those around me, laughing with
 and not at the expense of others.

May I let down my barriers of insecurity and pride,

allowing me the freedom to laugh at myself.

Let there be laughter in my heart, God!

Give me joy in my soul!

May it radiate like a beacon from me.

May it be evident in all I think, say, and do.

May it be a living testimony of your unconditional love.

Give me joy in my soul, God!

Put a smile on my face, laughter in my heart, and joy in my soul.

May your light shine brightly through me!

Amen

Use my gifts along the way.

Use my gifts along the way.

God Given Gifts

Almighty God, the giver of all gifts, the giver of life itself, reveal to me my gifts from you.

Awaken in me the desire to dig deep within my
  soul and discover a treasure that lies dormant,
    waiting to be unearthed and used.

Keep me from merely "scratching the surface" of the vision
  you have for my life.

Illuminate my heart that I might see the special tools you have
  instilled within me to be your disciple.

Open my eyes to your leading through those around me.

Grant me a spirit of acceptance, not denial; willingness, not apathy;
  trust, not disbelief.

Almighty God, the giver of all gifts, the giver of life itself,
  empower me to use my gifts from you.

Cast away all my fears and enable me to boldly move forward
  for you.

Let me perform wondrous works in your name, with the realization

that the seemingly small acts we do are often the greatest.

Forgive me when I compare my gifts with those of others.

Forgive me when I attempt to use these God-given gifts

for my own glory and not yours.

Almighty God, giver of all gifts, giver of life itself, you are the source

of all I am and hope to be.

Without you, I am like an empty vessel; visible,

but lacking substance and any true purpose of life.

But when I allow you to work through me,

what inner peace and joy I find!

Almighty God, to you be the glory!

Amen

*Focus on God
along the way.*

God at the Center

Dear God,

Worldly values clamor for my attention and draw me away from you.

The goals of "biggest" and "best" loom before me.

Success seems defined by the number of material things in one's possession and the position of importance one holds.

The path to good fortune looks paved with greed, self-centeredness, and apathy.

Temptation cries out to all, and sin appears to be watered down and ignored with a flood of excuses.

Redirect my gaze from earthly things,
and let my thoughts dwell on you.

Forever instill within me that the greatest treasure is often found in the smallest of vessels.

Impress on my heart that success is far better measured

by what we choose to give away rather than how much

we have accumulated.

Let me remember that good fortune is not attained by

walking over others but by walking beside them.

Deafen my ears to the temptations calling out to me, and grant me

a clear, not clouded, awareness of my sins.

Oh, Lord, turn my thoughts towards you!

Fill me with a deep yearning to accomplish your will.

Focus my whole being on your son, Jesus, who came that I might

have life and have it abundantly!

Amen

*Seek to know others
along the way.*

Seek to know others along the way.

Open My Eyes

Lord,
    Give me the desire to truly know my neighbors.
Sharpen my vision and enable me to look beyond
  surface appearances and see clearly who they are.
Let my view of them focus inward as well as outward.
Let my understanding encompass the whole person.
May I resist the temptation of "first impressions" and
  shallow relationships.
May I take the time to do:

      More listening and less talking
      More accepting and less judging
      More forgiving and less accusing
      More seeking and less ignoring
      More uplifting and less criticizing
      More them and less me

Give me the desire to truly know my neighbors.

May I see others as your children.

May I see others as you see them.

Open my eyes wide so that I can be your instrument in a world
   where people are longing to be seen and understood;
      crying out to be known and loved.

Amen

Look for rainbows
along the way.

Look for rainbows along the way.

Touch My Heart

Oh, God,
  Show me the rainbows in my life.
Make me aware of the light they bring to my
  moments and my days.
Touch my heart that I might feel the joyful message within.

Show me the rainbows in my life.
Impress on me their power to transform and renew.
Touch my heart that I might feel the hope they bring.

Show me the rainbows in my life.
Awaken me to the courage and strength to face my tomorrows.
Touch my heart that I might feel the faith they exude.

Show me the rainbows in my life.
Reveal to me the special blessings that are mine.
Touch my heart that I might feel your precious gifts of love.

Show me the rainbows in my life.

Splash their vibrant colors before me.

Touch my heart that I might overflow with praise and
thanksgiving for my God.

Touch my heart that my life would become a rainbow
to others for you.

Amen

*Embrace change
along the way.*

Embrace change along the way.

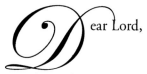

A Different Place

Dear Lord,

We have chosen to venture out to a different place.

We will be entering another stage of our lives.

We will be leaving the known, the familiar, the secure.

We are confronting change.

We have chosen to venture out to a different place.

Help us to embrace change and all the possibilities within it.

Give us a clear vision of the steps we need to take

to embark on this journey.

Loosen our grip on what is safe and comfortable,

that we may reach out to you in faith.

Grant us the courage and strength to face whatever

the future holds.

Let us forever remember that wherever we are,

you are there beside us; your love for us is everlasting

and unchanging.

Open wide our hearts to hold and carry with us all the
special memories we cherish so dearly.

Fill us with anticipation of dreams just waiting to unfold,
memories to be made, experiences to enrich our lives,
and people who will surely be a blessing to us.

In the midst of all our preparation, let us not forget to
truly live in the present and realize what a precious gift
each moment is.

We have chosen to venture out to a different place.

May your will be our will.

May all our actions reflect your love.

May each of us strive to be the person you created us to be.

We have chosen to venture out to a different place.

We lift up our thanks and praise to you Lord for change,
for the opportunity to grow, and for new beginnings!

We lift up our thanks and praise to you Lord
for your loving presence wherever life leads us.

Amen

*Let there be light
along the way.*

Let there be light along the way.

Light of Love

Lord Jesus,
      Let there be light in my life.
Let there be

Stars shining brightly in the night sky

Candles flickering in the darkness

The beautiful dawning of each new day

Sunlight peering over the graying clouds

A glowing fire to take away the cold

Let there be

Love of family, love of friends,

A thankful heart, a forgiving spirit,

Joy and laughter, faith and hope,

Moments to treasure, memories to share,

The desire to give, the humility to receive,

Peace in the midst of turmoil, courage in the presence of fear,

Let there be light in my life.

Let there be you, Lord Jesus, the light of the world!

Let there be light in my life.

Let it be you, Lord Jesus, who shines through me!

Amen

Find yourself along the way.

Find yourself along the way.

The Search

Dear Lord,
 I am seeking someone who seems
  to be hidden from me.

I call for this person to emerge and say, "Here I am!"

I reach out to touch and firmly grasp this person's hand.

I watch for signs that will give me a glimpse of where and who
  this person really is.

I carry a deep yearning within my heart to find myself.

My search is a lifelong journey.

A journey to discover the person you, Lord, created me to be;

A journey that draws me ever closer to you.

Lord, be my guide. Be my compass. Show me the direction
  I must take and help me not to stray from it.

Bring my true inner self out of the shadows and into the light.

Do not let this person forever elude me.

Instill within me the knowledge that I am unique and
   possess special gifts which you have given me.
Make me ever aware of these gifts that I may use them
   for your glory.
Take away all the useless clutter that fills my life
   and keeps buried all you would have me to become.
Remove any need I might have for the constant approval
   of others; replace it with the desire to please you.
Cast away all my fears and doubts and give me the courage
   to follow you wherever the path leads.
Do not let busyness take command of my life and smother
   the joy found in life's precious moments and the peace
   of just being.

May my age, stage, or status in life never keep me from pursuing
   my dreams.
Free me from comparing myself with others.
Release me from the sins of envy, resentment, judgment,
   and greed.
May painful memories and negative thoughts not be a hindrance
   to my journey.

Above all, help me to place you at the center of my life,

to keep your word ever before me, and to commune

with you daily.

Lord, I am seeking someone who seems to be hidden from me.

I call for this person to emerge and say "Here I am!"

I reach out to touch and firmly grasp this person's hand.

I am on a journey; a journey to find myself.

Each step is an act of faith.

Each step brings me closer to discovering the person you Lord,

created me to be .

Oh! Let me love that person.

Oh! Let me love myself.

For this is where the journey truly begins!

Amen

Honor our parents
along the way.

They Held My Hand

Lord,
They held my hand; guiding, supporting, loving.

They laughed with me, cried with me, rejoiced with me.

They sacrificed their needs for mine; giving both emotionally
and physically so that I could have.

They are my parents. They held my hand.

Now I am grown. The hands which held mine for so long
are growing weak.

Their strength is waning.

As each day passes, I watch the struggle to hold tight
to independence; to not be a burden.

Lord,

They are my parents. They held my hand.

Help me know how to reach out to them.

Instill within me the wisdom to discern their real needs.

Give me the ability to act and to be a loving presence in their lives.

Free me from unwarranted feelings of guilt and pressure
  I place upon myself.

Lord,

They are my parents. They held my hand.

It is now time for me to hold theirs.

How blessed I am!

Amen

Celebrate family along the way.

Celebrate family along the way.

The Gift of Family

Dear God,
 Praise and thanks to you for
 the gift of family!
Praise and thanks to you for
Hands held, hugs given,
Joys celebrated, burdens beared,
Tears shed, laughter shared,
Words to encourage, words to uplift,
Love when we are unlovable,
Forgiveness over and over again,
Times of togetherness,
Hope in the midst of despair,
Traditions made,
Memories to cherish,
Dreams fulfilled,
Moments of tenderness, moments of truth,
Prayers uttered,

A treasure to keep,

A place called home, a place to belong,

   a place of acceptance,

A circle of unending love.

May we never take family for granted.

May we rejoice that we are part of a family.

May we rejoice that we are each linked

   one with another, through the family of God!

Amen

*Set apart time for family
along the way.*

Set apart time for family along the way.

A Glimpse of Paradise

Dear Lord,

What a special occasion it was!

What a gift of love!

It was a time set apart for family.

A time when being together took the highest priority.

A time when each person released their grip on
personal agendas, schedules, and excuses.

A time when each person said, "Yes, we need to do this!"

What a special occasion it was!

What a gift of love!

It was a time set apart for family.

A time of sharing, laughing, and remembering.

A time of picture taking, hugging, and caring!

A time of breaking bread, worshiping, and rejoicing
with each other.

A time when each person said,

   "Yes, we need to do this more often."

What a special occasion it was!

What a gift of love!

It was a time set apart for family.

A time to keep in the memory book of our hearts.

A time that no amount of money could buy.

A time we will forever cherish and hold dear.

A time when each person said,

   "Yes, surely God is among us in this place!"

Lord,

What a special occasion it was!

What a gift of love!

It was a time set apart for family.

Perhaps it's in times like these that you reveal to us

   a glimpse of paradise.

Amen

*Appreciate one's heritage
along the way.*

Appreciate one's heritage along the way.

A Grateful Heart

Lord,
   I come before you with a grateful heart
for my heritage.

What a gift of love!

What a blessing it is!

Thanks be to you for my family,

A family that encircled me with their love, set a positive
   example, and created an atmosphere that allowed me
      to become the best I can be.

Thanks be to you for a family that exposed me to the Church
   and helped me to know you, Lord.

Thanks be to you for a family that valued spending time
   with each other; knowing this precious opportunity offers
      itself only once; knowing what they gave me could never be
         taken away.

Lord,

I come before you with a grateful heart for my heritage.

What a gift of love!

What a responsibility it is!

Help me to forever remember and cherish
   what was entrusted to me.

Keep me from diminishing the importance of its impact
   on my life.

Fill me with the deep desire to pass this heritage
   on to future generations.

Guide me in the understanding that this is the greatest legacy
   I can leave!

Lord,

I come before you with a grateful heart for my heritage.

What a gift it is!

What a blessing it is!

What a responsibility it is!

Thanks be to you for my family.

Thanks be to you, the source of "every good and perfect gift."

Amen

Make room for friends
along the way.

Make room for friends along the way.

Love of Friends

Lord,
   May I make room in my heart for friends.
May I be open to the wonderful blessings that the gift
   of friendship brings.
Keep me from the myriad of distractions that subtly pull me
   away from my friends.
Distractions defined by:
I am just too busy!
There is not enough time.
The distance is too great.
It is not "my turn" to call.
The house is not in order.
Maybe next week, month, year?
It is not my place to forgive.

Distractions that close, not open; constrict, not expand.
Distractions that crowd my heart with shallow excuses,

and close the door on lasting friendships.

Help me to see that these precious relationships need attention
and care to grow and thrive.

Give me the desire to nurture my friendships and the insight
to know that being a friend is a choice I choose to make.

Forever impress on me that a true friend is a treasure of
immeasurable worth, which the things of this world
cannot replace.

Fill me with gratitude for those friends you have enriched
my life with.

May I never forget that you are my greatest friend, Lord.

May I make room in my heart for you.

May I be open to the wonderful blessings that the gift
of your friendship brings.

May I live my life in joy and thanksgiving
for your everlasting love.

Amen

*Guide our children
along the way.*

A Prayer for Children

*L*ord,
　　We come before you in prayer for our children.
Help us to lovingly reach out, clasp their hands,
　　and draw them ever nearer to you.
Make us aware of the tremendous privilege and responsibility
　　we are entrusted with.
Guide us as we try to nurture our children's understanding
　　of what it means to pray.
Give us the ability to explore the Bible with our children
　　so that they may come to know you and your will
　　　　for their lives:
Instill within us ways to show our children an appreciation
　　for your world.
Awaken in us the need to become an active part of the
　　community of faith.
Impress on our hearts the importance of celebrating and sharing
　　special times together in the life of the church.

Fill us with your love so that we are able to embrace our children

during times of sadness, confusion, and doubt.

Help us to feel our children's trusting hands holding ours.

Help us as, hand in hand, we grow in faith together!

Amen

(From *Hand in Hand, Growing Spiritually with our Children,* by Sue Downing,

copyright ©1998 Discipleship Resources; page 5.)

Remember our schools
along the way.

A Place to Grow

Lord,

We give praise and thanks to you for our schools.

We pray that you continue to bless the very special ministry

they have been entrusted with.

Let every school be a learning place.

A place where each child is celebrated for who they are,

and the unique talents and gifts they have to offer.

Where children are encouraged to grow socially and emotionally,

as well as mentally.

Where teachers realize they are in the process of growing too,

for learning transcends all ages.

Lord, let our schools be a learning place.

Let every school be a laughing place.

A place where smiles abound, the sounds of laughter

can be heard, and fun fills the air!

Where happiness in what we are about is evident in all we do.

Where we discover joy in the everyday simple things;

a truth best taught by our children.

Lord, let every school be a laughing place.

Let every school be a listening place.

A place where we listen not only with our ears,

but with our hearts.

Where we genuinely hear the needs of our children

and each other.

Where we have the insight to know that to truly listen

to another is one of the greatest gifts we can give.

Lord, let our schools be a listening place.

Let every school be a loving place.

A place where you, Lord, are at the center of all we do.

Where our actions buildup, encourage, and give hope.

Where our lives are an expression of your will and love for us.

Lord, let our schools be a loving place.

Let our schools be a learning, laughing, listening,

   and loving place.

But foremost, Lord, let them each be a place where you dwell.

Amen

Have hope along the way.

Have hope along the way.

The Little Things

ear Lord,
As we journey through this Advent season,
help us to be ever mindful of your precious gift of hope.
Grant us the understanding that our greatest hope often
comes to us through the seemingly little things in life.

Amidst these days of preparation and anticipation,
open wide our hearts to recognize and receive hope
in treasured moments like:

The lighting of a candle, the smile of a child,
the love of a friend, the gathering of family,
a star filled sky, the open door of a church,
a time of prayer, the ringing of bells,
a hymn of praise and thanksgiving,
softly falling snowflakes, a first step taken,
the gentle nudge of the Holy Spirit.

Lord,

Amidst these days of preparation and anticipation,

   open wide our hearts to recognize and receive hope as we

      behold a manger in Bethlehem, that cradles a newborn baby,

      your son Jesus, the greatest hope of the world.

Amen

*Listen to the bells
along the way.*

Listen to the bells along the way.

Christmas Bells

Be still, listen, can you hear the
    bells of Christmas?
They sing out with joyful anticipation for the birth
    of the Christ child.
Their message is clear. Get ready, prepare the way,
    for Christ is coming; Christ is coming indeed!
Listen, it is time for our Advent journey to begin.

Be still, listen, can you hear the bells of Christmas?
They resound throughout our world, drawing us away
    from all the clamor and commercialism of the season.
The bells call us by name and invite us to reach out in love
    to one another.
Listen, it is time to focus our hearts towards Bethlehem.

Be still, listen, can you hear the bells of Christmas?
They whisper to us in the silence of a star-filled night.

We are being led to a manger in a lowly stable of Bethlehem.

Listen, it is time. The birth of Jesus is at hand.

Be still, listen, can you hear the bells of Christmas?

They herald the joyful news of hope to humankind.

With each toll, the bells proclaim, Christ,

   the son of God has come to be among us.

Love is born today!

Listen, it is time to give thanks and praise

   to almighty God for the greatest of gifts.

Be still, listen, can you hear the bells of Christmas?

They forever ring "Joy to the World!"

They forever ring within each one of us!

Amen

Go home along the way.

Go home along the way.

Lead Me Home

Lord,

This Advent season, help me to be still and listen
that I may hear your voice.

Lead me home to you.

Help me to discern your words in the midst of all the "glitz"
and commercialism of this world that "shout" out to me
and clamor for my attention.

Keep me from getting entangled within a web of busyness
that entraps me and leaves me feeling frustrated and empty.

Free me from the belief that material possessions provide
the answer for my happiness.

Lord,

This Advent season, help me to be still and listen,
that I may hear your voice.

Lead me home to you.

Let your message flow from those who are hurting
and have lost all hope.

May I be touched by the troubled and outcasts of this world.

Make me your instrument to help shatter the walls of hatred,
prejudice, and greed that exist in our world today.

Lord,

This Advent season, help me to be still and listen,
that I may hear your voice.

Lead me home to you.

Let me hear you in carols being sung, bells ringing,
and the laughter of children.

Make yourself known to me through the flickering of candles
and the beauty of a star filled sky.

Reach out to me in traditions made, gifts given, and joys shared.

Lord,

This Advent season, help me to be still and listen,
that I may hear your voice.

Lead me home to you.

Guide me to a place where a newborn baby lies in a manger;

A place where love, peace, and hope shine brightly;

A place where I discover anew your son Jesus,

    the light of the world!

Lord,

This Advent season, help me to be still and listen,

   that I may hear your voice.

Lead me home to you.

Instill in me that home is a place in my heart where you dwell.

Open my heart that I can receive the good news and know that

Christ is coming. Christ is coming indeed!

Joy to the world!

Amen

*Celebrate birthdays
along the way.*

Celebrate birthdays along the way.

Happy Birthday

Lord, it is my birthday.

Today I find myself acutely reminded of the
rapid passage of time.

Today I find myself almost unbelieving of the age
I have reached.

Today I pray for the wisdom to acknowledge your gifts of
love and grace for me.

Today I pray for a joyful and thankful spirit.

Lord, it is my birthday.

Help me not to gauge my life by the material possessions
I have accumulated, my status in the business world,
the social groups I belong to, the area where I live,
or my outward appearance.

Rather, let me count my blessings, and recall the times
I have reached out to others, and touched them
with your love.

Let me number the days I have spent doing your will

and using my God-given gifts for your glory.

Instill within me that faith, family, and friends

are what constitute the real essence of life.

Lord, it is my birthday.

Fill me with a yearning to seek out and focus on the good,

no matter what my circumstances.

May I savor my moments, and live a life that places

no age limits on living each day to the fullest.

Make me ever aware that my life is a gift, not an entitlement.

Grant me the ability to embrace hope and be a loving presence

to those around me.

Place within my heart the realization that it is not how long

I live, but how I live that gives true meaning to my life.

Lord, it is my birthday.

Today I celebrate my life.

Today I rejoice that I am a child of God!

Amen

Commit to love
along the way.

A Wedding Prayer

ord, we place this couple into your loving arms.

Instill within their hearts the gift of faith.

Let it be a growing faith that places you, Lord, at the very

center of their lives. Impress on them the understanding that

faith is their true foundation; for faith supports,

strengthens, and sustains.

It will uphold them throughout all the circumstances of life.

May these, your children, be united in faith as they are

united as one.

Lord, we place this couple into your loving arms.

We ask that you give them the precious gift of hope.

Impart to them the knowledge that hope is the promise of

things to come; for hope uplifts, gives purpose, and fills

our lives with meaning.

Hope lights our path.

May these, your children, be united in faith and hope,

as they are united as one.

Lord, we place this couple into your loving arms.

Grant each of them the gift of everlasting love.

Give them the awareness that love is the very essence of life

and without love we are nothing; for love "bears all things,

hopes all things, believes all things."

Let them always remember that the greatest gift we have to give

is our love.

May these, your children, be united in faith, hope, and love as

they are united as one.

Lord, we place this couple into your loving arms.

Hold them forever close and bless them today as they are

joined together through the holy sacrament of marriage.

Amen

*Celebrate new life
along the way.*

Celebrate new life along the way.

A Precious Miracle

What joy! What celebration! What wonder!
A new life is beginning!
A new life is making itself known within the shelter
of a mother's womb.
A new life, conceived in love; a gift of God.
A new life, unique from all others; a realization
of hopes and dreams.

Lord of life, Creator of all things,
Cradle this child in your loving arms.
Shelter this child, and hold it close.
Watch over each step of its forming, growing, and becoming.
Guide every movement it makes.

Lord of life, Creator of all things,
Wrap this child's parents in the warmth of your love.
Envelop them with the caring support of family and friends.

129

Give them thankful hearts for this very special time
   in their lives.
Walk with them and guide them as they experience
   the precious miracle that is a result of their love for each other.

What joy! What celebration! What wonder!
A new life is beginning!
We rejoice in the good news!
We lift our voices in praise and thanks to you God,
   the Lord of life and Creator of all things!

Amen

Printed in the United States
64279LVS00003B/76-147

9 781583 850848